Stripped Naked

"…Lest I strip her naked." Hosea 2:3

Brunetta Nelson

DEDICATION

I dedicate this book to the most loving parents - the late **Alphonzo Nelson, Sr., and Pastor Doris Virginia Hall-Nelson**, and my baby sister whom heaven has already claimed - **Sylvia Elaine Nelson**, my elder siblings, Tyrone & wife Kim, Debra & Gary, Alphonzo Jr., Barbara & husband-the late Stanley Hester, Angela, Antonio, our extended family Mattie and Treasure, my uncles Jerry, Sunny and Mason Hall, my only surviving aunt Catherine & husband Eddie, cousins, friends, associates and loved ones.

Senator Fort, Joe Beasley, Tim Franzen, all the demonstrators of Occupy Atlanta, Atlanta New Generation Ministries, Bishop Kevin White, Pastor Anthony Williams, Pastor Richard White, Sr., Ministers Steve & Teresa Deaton, Ronnie Allen, and everyone that has sown seeds of wisdom into my life - You are an amazing People and I thank God for you!

I also dedicate this book to the amazing women that were housed at **Fulton County Jail, Lee Arrendale Women's Prison, and the awesome women at Emanuel Women's Facility** during the time I was incarcerated. I met some of the most talented women in prison. It is striking and alarming how such smart, talented, and beautiful women find themselves behind prison bars. This fact is a major part of the driving force in me to help prevent as many as possible from going down this path. This experience has definitely set a fire in me, a burning passion and a genuine love that has changed me and the way I will serve in Kingdom Building. I was so inspired and touched by many of your stories, experiences, and your kindness towards me. God allowed me to meet, minister and learn from so many diverse personalities and cultural differences. I was so honored to serve and lead many of you to Christ who are now members and serving in the body!

I will never forget the executive staff, counselors, and the officers at Emanuel Women's Facility. I refer to them as **"Women In Power."** I love it! I was so grateful to have those smart, confident, and focused women to be responsible for me. There was not a day I didn't hope to be home while in prison, but if I had to be in a prison, Emanuel was definitely the place. **Warden Mickens** surely filled the tall order her position required. She also made us feel like she cared for us and that she wanted not only a successful program, but also for us to re-enter society successfully as productive citizens. I'm grateful that she was open to allow me access to the Career Center daily to begin writing this book. And Sargent Holland, who was the officer at the Career Center while I was there, encouraged us and always gave us a warm smile.

I look forward to sharing my prison experience in detail in the next book. This book is an introduction to the five book series focusing on **Shame, Silence, and Secrets**. I desire to be transparent, vulnerable, and free from disguise to share my life experience. I want to use all of this as a vehicle to bring awareness, encouragement, and understanding to move many in the right direction. Stay with me. This will be an unforgettable journey!

CONTENTS

CONTENTS (CONT.)

ACKNOWLEDGMENTS

The first acknowledgment and recognition goes to The Keeper, Lover, and Sustainer of my soul, the all-powerful, all knowing, infinite Father-Daddy and my everything, God the Father, God the Son, and God the Holy Spirit, the Sovereign and Almighty Jehovah. He is the source of my very life and the origin of this book. I'm learning to love and lean on Him with every fiber of my existence, even when He chastises me. God, You are Sovereign, there's none like You, beneath, above or on the earth, in this life or the life to come! Those that labored in prayer for me in the United States, other countries and continents, I am so humbled by your willingness to remember me in prayer.

The Kairos Prison Ministries Organization - for serving in God's vineyard through spiritual retreats that are life changing. Your presence and example of God's love changed my life! You inspired me at the darkest hour of my life. No one but the loving Father could have placed you in my path at such a perfect time. My heart was literally on its last beat and in desperate need for a breath of fresh air! You poured God's love into me like a Niagara-fall and caused a spiritual resuscitation that would not let me die. I've had spiritual freedom since. You are a blessed people. Your example is what the church should look like. I will never forget all of you!

Bishop T.D. Jakes - who has inspired me through his gifted teaching and preaching abilities from Heaven. You are my TV evangelist that spoke much life and encouragement to me at the most difficult time and place in my life. I pray that your voice will travel in the untapped places in the earth so that those who want to give up will stand up as the dead bones did in Ezekiel's vision. Your book, *Naked But Not Ashamed*, awakened some dead places in my life. Your title was so close to the title of this book that I hesitated to read it before finishing the manuscript. Many were already referring to me as a little female T.D. Jakes. I am glad I read it because your words compelled me to go back to my childhood to see some things that are important for such a time as this. God bless you, and keep inspiring us!

Pastor Andy Stanley - *The Principle of The Path* is the book that is just what the Almighty God ordered for me. It changed my life in an instance! I now understand that even a book can be a divine appointment, and God gives us what we need only when we are ready. Reader, you don't want to miss how some of Pastor Stanley's ideas are so applicable to our lives! It's a must read!

Author Nancy Alcorn - *Echoes of Mercy & Ditch The Baggage (Change Your Life)* You are amazing! Your book lifted my thoughts. It raised my ability to trust and to obey the Lord to an entirely new level. I am so grateful that you paused for a moment just for me. I am more than inspired to pay your compassion forward in this journey called life! Thank you and may the Lord bless you.

Author David Herzog - *Mysteries of The Glory Unveiled* - God purposed me to read your book at the appointed time. I had no idea what I was about to experience or learn, but I knew the book was commissioned by God. While reading this book, I felt as though I was learning at the speed of light. Wisdom, knowledge and understanding were crammed into me with great purpose. The author stated, "Although Paul was in chains, it did not diminish his authority!" Wow! I remember walking into prison and feeling for some time that the authority God had given me as His servant was limited. What a revelation and a jolt in my spirit. At that moment, I believe I leaped as John did in Elizabeth's womb! I want to personally thank you for sharing such personal, moving experiences, and revelations about this amazing area of ministry.

Pastor Timothy McBride - Tabernacle Of Praise Church International On June 24, 2018, sitting in your early morning service, God used the beginning of your series, *Restoration*, to jumpstart my restoration process. I was finally home from prison. I love mornings and could not wait to attend the early morning service. I was blown away because God had called me to a 30-day restoration and recuperation journey before I would begin my new assignments as a free woman. Initially I asked, "God, how will I fit in? Should I wait to set up the new ministry? How God? I am ready for Kingdom business beyond any scale I've ever known." When you opened your mouth, I heard your love for Jesus! I immediately identified with your spirit and I said to myself, he's a smiler just like I am. Thank you for your obedience to begin the series on *that* day.

Let me also take a moment to acknowledge all of those that "pushed" me into my destiny. Whether it was intentional or by happenstance, you were strategically positioned and purposed for the perfect assignment and time. For that I say thank you. May God touch and bless everyone that has come in and out of my life, - the good, the bad, and the ugly - for the Lord gets all the glory, and nothing shall be wasted. I am often reminded of the words of the anonymously penned work that says, *"People come into your life for a reason, a season, or some for a lifetime!"* I'm so, so grateful, privileged, and blessed to share this moment with you!

Again, a special thanks to **Pastor Anthony Williams**, I love you and **First Lady Williams**. Thank you both for welcoming me into your home and loving me as a part of your family. **Mr. Ronnie Allen**, you are a true friend and an example for all of us, especially me. **Bishop Alphonzo White, Sr.**, you never stopped praying for me, thank you. **Tabitha Cline** we are sisters for life. **Nancy, Cindy,** and **Teresa**, I am so grateful to have met you. You all are angels from above! Keep inspiring us!

FOREWORD

Around the summer of 2014, I met Brunetta. We were connected during a catastrophic event she and her sisters (Angela, and the baby girl, the late Sylvia Elaine Nelson) were experiencing relative to their business and real estate. When I learned about their story, my compassion grew greater. Their small business was being bullied by a local bank, the small business they had built brick-by-brick for over 20 years.

The existence of a 20 year plus certified "Minority Female Owned Construction Business" in the heart of East Point brought its own uniqueness. I had walked with many businesses before, but to meet these ladies that were blood sisters, close-knitted, passionate about the construction industry, and view their love and respect for one another was impressive.

As I reflect over the initial time and interaction with Brunetta during her tremendous test of faith, the bank's behavior didn't surprise me. I committed to walking with her and her sisters just as I had walked with others. Their business held the noteworthy designation as a certified and licensed MBE, FBE, LSBE, WOSB, AABE, Lead & Asbestos, Weatherization, RRP remodeling government contractor. The firm was owned and operated from its very own commercial office complex, and had an impeccable record performing government contracts within its expertise.

Let me say this book is perhaps one of a kind. It's rare that a devout Christian, Pastor, Community Leader, and Entrepreneur puts it all on the line to go deep to share her mistakes with real talk and transparency. Brunetta desires to share her discoveries in the rawest form in order to help others. She strongly believes that there needs to be "real talk" about what happens when we think our back is against the wall and we feel that there is nowhere to turn, as well as the value of keeping with principle. She is passionate about sending the message to others to not respond with desperation when a crisis or critical event occurs in life. Brunetta wants to make a difference for people that find themselves in the place of "shame, silence, and secrets." As she reflects in *Stripped Naked*, Brunetta has made some choices that resulted in great consequences. Her desire is that the price she has paid will not just move her forward in wisdom, experience, understanding, principal, and truth, but she hopes to prevent others from making the same mistakes she has made.

When I think of some challenges in my own life, it's amazing how what we view as the worst thing that can ever happen can be a great push and breakthrough to get us closer to our destiny. I see the heart Brunetta has for ministry, particularly young people. I've had an opportunity to share moments with Brunetta as she spoke very passionately about her desire to help others avoid the mistakes she made. I particularly like that Brunetta took full responsibility for her actions. She wrote this book with the desire to bring freedom to everyone that wants to be free from "shame, silence and secrets."

During the fight of her life to save her business, its status, the accumulations of real estate, and all that comes with over 20 years in business, Brunetta was committed to stand with others to help them fight for freedom from any form of bondage, as well as helping others obtain victory. Brunetta pours her heart out in her book. She literally shares very personal and intimate moments about her own life. She wants to start the conversation that will help many to break through and find that freedom that she has found. The book is the first of a "five book series" with the steps *to your freedom!*

Finally, Brunetta, I pray that God will use your experience to touch the lives of many. I am so proud to see this book project become a reality. Keep pressing toward the mark for the prize of the high calling of God in Christ Jesus!

God bless you,

The Honorable Joe Beasley
Civil Rights Activist

TO THE TEAM FROM THE AUTHOR

Ladies I am in awe as I ponder over the tireless nights and days we have shared to produce this project! Your love, compassion, and dedication is impressive. I will always be grateful to you. Olivia and Patience, we have spent a year with the manuscript. We shared every emotion as we worked tireless hours together. I loved the times God moved us into worship together in the midst of working on the manuscript. The power of three. Every one of you rock and this project is successful because of you!

Chief Editor - Pastor Patience Rose of Red Worldwide, Inc.
Lead Writing Coach - Olivia Gibbs of Imprint Productions, Inc.
Photography & Cover - Amelia Warrener of A.W. Consulting
Prayer Intercessor - Teresa Deaton of Heart 4 Worship Ministries

I love you guys!

There is no coincidence that this book is in your hands. You're about to get naked! All of your senses (body, mind, and spirit) must hear the words of this book. Get ready, the curtain is about to open! You might have to (in police lingo...) "assume the position." No, I'm not talking about just raising your hands over your head, leaning against a wall, and being frisked. I'm talking about taking off all your clothes, spreading your cheeks, bending over, and coughing. No, I'm not talking about enlisting in the military. This is an involuntary army, the disarmed forces where your name, rank, and serial number become your inmate identification number. This is the "Big House," "Down the River," where your worst nightmare has come true. While I'm not asking you to literally take your clothes off, I want your commitment to be naked, opened, and vulnerable while you take this walk with me. You will get the most out of this walk if you agree to be unguarded. I want you to ditch the thoughts that will impede your mind at this moment.

The weight of *shame* can be lifted. The *silence* can be broken. You can be free from the secrets that keep you awake at night, if you desire. Walk with me! Decide to face yourself. This is where it starts! You can denounce everything that keeps you from moving towards your victory. Don't allow the deception of untruth to keep you from holding your head up and looking at those you talk to in the eye. My hope is to inspire you to break free from the *shame, silence,* or *secrets* that have imprisoned you or someone connected to you. I was forced to do it, but if you embrace our moments together in the freedom of truth and victory, you will love yourself again greater, and love others more than ever before!

Commit to our time together. We will take Twelve Simple Steps that will transform your life and change how you see yourself, just as they changed me. Let's get to it!

❧ CHAPTER 1 - STRIPPED NAKED

Sometimes everything must come off! Just recently, I decided that I needed to get my body in order. I really wanted to lose 20 pounds in 20 days! So I started at the gym. Time met opportunity at 6:15 a.m. the next day. I went into the gym and gave those machines everything I had for 60 full minutes! When I finished, I had nothing left. I was hot, sticky and exhausted! I needed a bath. With my clothes full of perspiration and my skin layered in sweat, I was compelled to get naked so that I could take full advantage of the hot, relaxing, refreshing bath that was to come.

About five years ago now, I found myself in a hot, sticky, sweaty mess. Everything in my life was layered and I longed for the refreshing that God had in store. Let me paint a picture for you... imagine old wood with layers of peeling paint. In my business, we restored crown molding, baseboards, and door trim. Most of the time we have to strip the wood completely before we can restore it with a beautiful high gloss perfected finish. The process is very tedious. Its meticulous nature requires patience, planning and tender loving care. The remarkable thing about the process is that as the designer, I could see the finished product even when it was in its most deteriorated state. This is the Master Designer's creative art. He knows what is required to make us, to perfect us, and restore us to our original beauty. Stripping...the harsh process of working layer by layer, peeling off, scraping off, stripping away everything that does not look like the finished product... Ouch, what a painful and sometimes humiliating experience for us. My hot, sticky mess found me stripped naked before the Lord for a time of reparation, and it's really the best thing that could have ever happened to me to correct my abnormalities, deterioration, and irregularities. The lack of upkeep causes decay and over time the decay works its way into every crack and crevice. When this happens, stripping is really the only method to restore completely. God's tough love was lifesaving. It opened my eyes and placed me back on the right path! Stripping is exactly what God did to me!

God has a perfect plan for everyone but His perfect plan for me was to include so much more than I could see at the time. He had to peel away the pride I had in my business. He had to strip my position in the community and the reputation I had built in my image. That includes all the properties, all those certifications and distinguished designations I had amassed. Many times we start out with great purpose and good intentions but we end up building our kingdom instead of His. You know those areas that you protect from any criticism... areas that you guard like they're your own? You say it's for God, your community or others, but you know it's really for you.

I must say, I am so grateful that He loved me enough to chastise me in a way that only He could. When my siblings and I became adults, our mother told us that, after she disciplined us, she would enter her room and cry. I can imagine God crying especially when His child messed up like I did. My "mess" landed me in prison, and when I arrived, I was so humiliated when they told me to strip naked. We were gifted an ugly white jumpsuit, granny panties - one size fits most, Timberland Knock-off boots that ensured that all arches were no longer in force, and a one-way trip straight to the shower. We were given strong smelling shampoo to put in our hair to kill lice and we had to stand there in the cold for 15 minutes to make sure it worked. In the spiritual realm after God stripped me, He had to wash me. When the dirty clothes are taken off, the body is still dirty, so a bath comes before you put on the new clothes. God had to exchange my clothes of desperation, deception and destruction for His clothes of truth, trust and tested. Exactly! He stripped me, washed me, clothed me in His own garments and now I am clean! I'm clean and cleared of my past. It can no longer pollute me, nor hold me hostage.

Now that I was clean, God could begin to divinely position me in a place that would ultimately expand the ministry and equip me with the tools I needed to be effective. There are people assigned to our lives that we will meet in some of the most unexpected places. The plan was set in place before we were formed in our mother's womb! God is so amazing! He never makes mistakes! Now, when my feet hit the floor in the mornings, the devil cringes because Jehovah will allow *me* to inspire, encourage, and win souls for the body of Christ! I am persuaded, compelled and elevated! I am now moving forward powerfully in the assignment that was my intended purpose from the Lord. What the devil meant for bad, God has made it good!

Listen, I was ashamed, secretive and scared. I cried every morning because I knew I was caught in a net and I couldn't see the end. To be totally honest, I never meant to hurt anyone. I thought money would solve my problem, but I know now that money was not the solution. That's why God shut down the resources. Instead of performing maintenance on the cancer, God removed it. What an excruciating method, but He knows what's best for us.

My prison experience was a result of my acts of desperation and poor judgment that propelled me to alter invoices and leverage them to borrow money for thirty days. Floating funds with altered documents is the same as stealing funds (just for a shorter time frame), and in my desperate state, I could not process that. It was never my intention to take or keep the money. I'm so glad that everything in me was exposed because I didn't see the warning signs. I was *wrong* for it all and there is *never* an excuse to do wrong. In my renewed mind, I believe in my heart that I could have explained what I was facing and what I was trying to achieve to the person I victimized. This would have given him the opportunity to help me.

The meltdown, the breakdown, the crash that I experienced and the catastrophic results that followed, cost me everything - not to mention years of earned trustworthiness and displayed integrity. I begged God to deliver me and I even gave Him instructions on how I wanted Him to do it. I now know that God answered my prayers, but He did it His way. I received His deliverance while incarcerated at Emanuel Women's Facility. He cleansed me of many things that I never knew I had tucked inside me while He used me to bring about deliverance and salvation to many of the women who were right alongside me.

On the day I surrendered myself to the custody of Fulton County Jail, I was still looking for some divine intervention from God. Looking back, He had given me so many opportunities, but I had not passed that "trust" test that was required for God to override prison time. A few days before I was in court with my lawyer, he had entered a motion to allow me more time to work something out, but I panicked. I had the anxiety attack of the century. As a result of that episode, I acquired a roundtrip ticket to the emergency room and I never saw the judge that day. I simply did not trust God. Even though God had shown Himself trustworthy many times before, my lack of trust was overwhelming. In that moment, I clearly heard God speak to my spirit, "You must learn to *trust* me." I later learned that the judge would have given me a chance if I had just trusted God.

There is something about God! He loves us so much that He knows when we need more love, especially when we are disobedient and are in need of correction. During my fifth month in prison, I learned to trust God on a deeper level. Up until that point, I had been trying to hold on to everything I could and control it all… even from prison. Most of us can trust Him for others but we must learn to trust Him for ourselves. In that moment, I finally released everything to Him. He showed me how and why I must trust Him. It seems as though I had Him all to myself. Our God is multitasking at all times on all fronts with all of His children, because we are His!

Step 1: Be Truthful

☙ CHAPTER 2 - THE DETOUR

In early 2014, I was in our corporate offices on the corner of Harris and Normanberry Drive in East Point, Georgia. I was the Chief Executive Officer of one of the few female double minority certified, licensed contractors in the country with 25 years of experience. Several of the largest contractors in the city contacted me hoping to cross off two requirements for 17% of federally funded contracts: minority and female. I am looking out of the window of my corner office. I am not in a penthouse, but this is *my* top of the world. I am respected in the community. I am leading as senior Pastor at my church. I am the President of DBABS Construction, Inc., but my personal life is a private mess.

No one can see through my confident facade that I am fighting for my life. The bank is trying to foreclose on my buildings, including our Corporate Office Complex. I've exhausted every source of cash flow, reserves, and emergency funds to fight them. This bank that had been my lending source, is now my enemy. I am finally down to the last $12,000 payment to the *specialized* lawyer representing us in our fight against the bank who assures me he is David to their Goliath. I haven't done any new business in nearly a year because I've been so focused on fighting for the life of my 25 year empire. Now my back is against the wall and resources are few.

At this juncture, I am exposed and open for any solution. Not only am I desperate, I am lost. Suddenly in my pursuit of ideas, I thought to myself, "if I can get enough funds to defeat the bank in court, I can recoup all of the money spent, redeem my relationships, and the money would put everything back into perspective." I can identify more than ever with the woman with the issue of blood. I was thinking, "if I can just touch enough money, I know I will be made whole!" There's only one catch: it's illegal, but I know it will work. I know it will tide me over: I will change the dates on some invoices and leverage them as collateral to get me to the finish line. I have contracts that are being paid soon, so I will be able to get the money back before my lie gets exposed. Money will start coming in within 30 days. Somehow it will all come together. It always does. I know it's illegal but I will pay it back. The investor knows me. We have history. We've done multiple deals, in fact we have other deals generating revenue now. If anything goes wrong, he knows I will pay him back. I have too much to lose not to pay him. He will understand. I say it in my mind a hundred times, added to the hundred more. I say it again. It's Friday, I am convinced that this transaction is right. I silence the voice in my head that keeps saying this is wrong on all levels, regardless of my good intentions to pay it back.

"Why can't I sleep?" I say as I wake up at 3:00 in the morning. It's Saturday… but sleep refuses to come. My heart pounds and pains as I face the woman in the mirror that knows she has done a terrible thing! I can't run away from myself. The heaviest conviction fell on me. I know right from wrong. My mother was a woman of faith. She feared God and had taught us to do the same. My daddy was an honest man. Every time the church door was opened, I was there. When Mama preached, I was there with her and hanging on her every word while playing the drums. And when the choir sang, I would direct them. There are consequences to your actions. "You can't get away with doing wrong," she preached loud and long. She had the strap to back it up, i.e., she didn't spare the rod of chastisement. After receiving two of her "chastisements," I quickly learned that I didn't want another one. No matter how hard I cried, it never stayed the tide of those strokes with that belt or the switches. "It's going to be alright," I told myself the thousandth time, "I will replace the money in 30 days."

The stakes were so high. I remember wishing I could close my eyes and every mistake I had made would just go away. Inadvertently, in my own effort to be the greatest servant of God I could be, I got lost. My tenacious drive to run for Jesus got distorted and I ran right past Him. I was running so fast that it took being incarcerated in prison for three years for Him to catch up with me. The police actually came to my office to get me and I was still answering phone calls. I was busy! I remember walking to the main entrance of our building proudly to ask what I could help them with. When they said, "Brunetta Nelson," and showed me their badges, I was paralyzed. I would have turned myself in, I said. Truth is, I thought I had more time to make this lie right. You can't. They cuffed me right in front of my staff. I suddenly knew that everything I feared was happening. My big secret was coming out. My reputation, my business, my ministry, my empire all on fire, and I was the arsonist! The *shame, silence,* and *secret* would come to an end.

There is no force more relentless than the Holy Spirit when you have a call on your life. My call is Kingdom business and Kingdom building ministry. My worst nightmare occurred at one of the most fascinating times of my life. Proud as a peacock, at the helm of two of the loves of my life; DBABS Construction, Inc. and Atlanta New Generation Ministries, Inc., I was the founder of them both, from the cradle. After my writing coach, Olivia, read this sentence she said, "I could literally visualize you in the cradle founding these two organizations. You are holding the Articles of Incorporation like the 10 Commandments." I was born to do business! Kingdom Business, here I come! No, I wasn't interested in playing with dolls; but I wasn't climbing trees either. I played monopoly and won every time.

At 15 years old, I knew I wanted to have my own business, so my sister, Sylvia, and I started a fashion business and named it B&S Unique. We hired models to provide fashion shows featuring our original designs during birthday parties, luncheons, and other special events. The models were sometimes older than us. We were rich when we got paid $100.00, and we then paid our models. Yes, I was born to do business.

When I was at Columbia School Of Broadcasting, I would record my audio stories about business people. I can hear my recordings as I am writing: Donald Trump and his junk bonds back in the 1980's; John Portman and his architectural designs, particularly The Westin at Peachtree Street in Atlanta, featuring the first rotating restaurant on top of 86 floors (which became a signature design for Westin); and the ultimate, Mr. H.J. Russell becoming the nation's first largest black-owned construction and real estate company blew me away! He was right here in Atlanta! I remember thinking, "That's it! I am going to be a millionaire!" I knew something greater was calling me, I just didn't know the steps to get there. At 17, you don't know that you don't know.

My first dream was to become a Fortune 500 business owner. I remember making the announcement to my mother, a couple of close associates, and my daddy that I would be a millionaire at the age of 25. I was working in private banking temporarily as an Administrative Assistant/Receptionist. I was interacting with millionaires that called to have hundreds and millions of dollars wire transferred by just a phone call or dropping by the office. "What a cool thing," I thought as an ambitious young woman, "a section of the bank just for them!" That was exciting to me. This exposure helped to shape my vision of my millionaire status to come - a preview of a coming attraction!

I knew that this millionaire status would not come by way of working for someone. I remember stepping onto a construction site to see an existing structure that was deteriorated beyond repair. The contractor allowed me to follow the revitalization of that house. This was the most fascinating thing I had ever witnessed! That house became new again. I remember deciding that construction and reconstruction was something I wanted to do - to take something at its worst condition and give it life again. I believe God was setting me up then, as I think about it. What a correlation in how He takes us just as we are and makes us new!

Finally, I had fallen in love with renovation, restoration, and refurbishing existing structures. Out of all the possible businesses available to pursue, it's ironic that a woman who loves heels, skirts, and dresses would choose to walk out her dream in a male- dominated industry. The more I visited the sites, the more I felt like I belonged. I remember talking to Sylvia about it. We brainstormed and Sylvia suggested we name the company DBABS which consisted of the first initials of each of the names of my sisters from the oldest to the youngest: Debra, Barbara, Angela, Brunetta, and Sylvia! DBABS Construction Inc. was born, and we officially incorporated the firm in 1995.

It was tough from the beginning. On the first day of a roofing job, one of the laborers said, "No bitch is going to tell me what to do." Yep, I had to set an order, a precedent, therefore I instructed my site manager to pay him and fire him. From that point, men would whisper to themselves. I would drive my shiny new black truck to the construction sites and step out wearing my pumps and miniskirts. I was determined to remain feminine and classy, my "MO." Even when I played basketball at Washington High School, as soon as I got off the court, I wore my tight jeans and my pumps. I remember in an article that was written about me and our business that I said, "I don't look like a man; I don't smell like a man, and I will not carry that 2x4 up the ladder like a man." I wasn't about to change me because I wanted to run a business in what was perceived as a "man's field." My unique ability as a female to bring the workforce, material supply, funding and project management was without equal. My position as a certified female- owned business was a small niche in high demand.

God made me female for this purpose.

Most people thought I was ahead of my time and my thinking off the charts. I was flattered. I didn't realize it then, but this is a tragedy. If there is no one who shares your dreams, no one speaking into your life, or you have no one in your circle that has done or is doing what you desire to do, you need to find someone! You cannot do this alone! The enemy loves to see you by yourself trying to work everything out in your head. He loves the Unholy Trinity: Me, Myself and I. There is nothing new under the sun. Someone has been there, done that, and has the t-shirt to prove it. Open your eyes. Look for it. They might be wearing that shirt today and you'd never notice if you aren't looking! I needed someone who was successful in both business and ministry to help me navigate. Because I am a black woman, it would be easy to say I needed a black female, but this transcends race. Don't allow yourself to be limited. You might miss your mentor because they don't look like you. I'm so glad God expanded my vision. It wasn't always so. Let Him expand yours too.

Step 2: Find yourself a Mentor, find a Coach, or find an Adviser that has achieved your goal, or is at a minimum actively doing the work.

ೞ CHAPTER 3 - COURSE CORRECTION

It is true that God's anointed men and women make bad choices and it is the design of the enemy to use the results of those choices to cause excruciating pain and sorrow that will impact everyone in our path. Believers are held to a higher standard (rightfully so), and being human is no excuse because to whom much is given, much is required. As the Senior Pastor of an amazingly progressive "NOW GENERATION" ministry of young people that was soaring like nothing I have ever seen, my consciousness, sensitivity and awareness of the evils that desired to bring me to a place of defeat dwindled. Being desensitized caused me to become spiritually indifferent. Seeing so many young people wanting to serve the Lord despite being labeled a "lost generation," made me want to do so much as a minister, but somehow I got lost! In nine months of ministry we more than doubled in size and kept growing. And just as this baby was being born, I was incarcerated. I thought surely God would not allow me to go to prison. I thought those babies required the nurturing only *I* could give.

I did not remain conscious of the enemy soldiering up against me when I became a threat to his kingdom. The enemy is a pedophile who wants each of us most when we're young. Transforming the lives of young people is one of the greatest threats to his kingdom. We must remain mindful to set up our garrisons against him, especially when dealing with the young. He wants to kill us anyway but this multiplies when we are preparing our young people for Christ.

We say a lot of things, but how we act shows what we really believe. The pressure in my business life began to impact my ministry. I didn't want anyone to know what I was facing. I thought I could handle it, so I started making decisions without prayer. I should have known I was in trouble when I didn't even want to look in the bible for confirmation. This was not the time to take up the old habit of forging ahead. In fact, I ended up serving time when I decided to follow my mind. Please hear this: you are going to serve somebody. You are going to either serve God, serve Satan, or serve yourself. Answer these questions if you don't know who you are serving: Will it bring money? Will it bring fame? Will it glorify God?

The bible makes it clear. A man cannot serve two masters. Man must choose one master: God or mammon. Mammon is money. So if the answer is money, you are serving satan. I know. That sounds really hard, but the bible instructs us that when we know the truth we will be set free. If you are serving money, you are not free. Mammon drives you. You can feel the pressure. It speaks to you when you're sleeping. You can never truly relax. Even when you drink alcohol in order to sleep, you will wake up at some crazy hour thinking about your deals.

If you're serving yourself, your pride gives you great pictures of how you will be recognized for your great contributions. Your illegal actions will be drowned out by your lofty dreams of cheering crowds who are applauding your accomplishments... you dream that you are receiving the Congressional Medal of Honor, a Nobel Prize, that you are the most requested speaker, that your book is a bestseller, the lofty dreams may be never ending. Just know that pride is driving your efforts and Self is on the throne. You are serving the Unholy Trinity: Me, Myself and I. Maybe you don't agree. I know - denial is usually the first response. Maybe you're thinking, "This is my contribution to mankind." I know. I know. But is it for *The King*? These are all worthy aspirations but when you're being driven to achieve these goals by money, it's not God. God leads us to green pastures. There is peace and we can sleep.

I didn't know I was being driven. A lot of pastors drive their sheep. What do I mean? When a pastor stands in the pulpit and commands you to do something that your conscience does not agree with, like giving a hundred dollars and saying you won't get blessed if you don't, that's not leading. That's driving. When opposition strikes that pins your back against the wall, that threatens everything you've worked for, your empire, your legacy, your reputation, your image, or maybe even your man or womanhood, what will you do? This is the defining moment. What is your familiar action, your old reaction or what comes natural when tragedy hits? Get this: Familiar reactions, or I call them habits, will show up, such as:

- Lying
- Avoiding the conversation because you don't want to lie
- Deliberately omitting pieces of your answers
- Purposely leaving out parts that might kill the deal or make matters worse
- Thinking "they didn't ask me so I didn't say anything" knowing full well that the info was necessary and should be included

Lay it all on the table up front - best feeling ever! Nothing is worth the loss of integrity. It's the little things that you have to pay attention to. Don't miss them, *they matter*. Learn from my mistakes, as I am willing to be transparent in sharing to help you. Of course, I am still experiencing a level of pain and remorse that could cause me to be grief stricken. Oh, but the merciful and loving Father that knows the ending before the beginning still loves me and I know He still has a plan for me! This book is a part of that plan.

To live in Him is to live by His principles. Watch your walk, words, and your ways. Never violate His principles because it is true that what you sow, you shall reap, good or bad. He requires us to be accountable and to endure the consequences of our actions. I'm so glad He corrected my course. We cannot manipulate God.

The bible declares that God chastens whom He loves. He must love me a whole lot because He whipped me butt naked. I created my mess and couldn't pray my way out, neither was sorry enough. The endless tears and remorseful feelings and thoughts were not enough. Sometimes the stakes are too high and we must face the consequences so that we can be corrected! God is too vested in your life to let you continue going the way you are going!

He will correct us while in the midst of dispensing His mercy and grace. I won't go back! King David who committed murder, Jacob who deceived, and Moses who murdered and ran away to avoid prosecution are perfect examples of people who were beneficiaries of God's mercy. They embraced God's correction and as a result received His mercy. I want you to know no matter what you have done, there is still mercy for you. God's grace will meet you where you are.

God will use you in your circumstances to bring humility and discovery that will push you into your destiny. I declare that destiny is awaiting your arrival! There will be dark, hard, and lonely places in your journey sometimes, but goodness and mercy will follow you. So stop saying the devil is behind you because he isn't. Goodness and mercy is. While incarcerated, I couldn't pastor the flock God had given me at Atlanta New Generation, but He gave me women at Emanuel Women's Facility, some who had never walked into a church. He showed me how to put them to work in the ministry and they were amazed at how right it felt. They never considered themselves "church" material and yet they prayed, sang in the choir, danced, ushered, wrote newsletters, and found their place. They finally felt accepted by God and His people.

The steps of a righteous man are ordered of the Lord, especially when it seems that they're not. I experienced God making holy what I thought wasn't holy and making righteous those who I thought weren't righteous. He transformed me from sometimes being a Pharisee to truly seeing Jesus in everyone. He gave me His heart. Now when I look at our world, I see people that were created uniquely by God - some may be of different color, some may have tattoos or piercings, some may have different color hair (red, gray, black, blue, pink...), some may wear suits and ties, and some may wear jeans and t-shirts - but ALL were created by our Loving God, and *I can see Jesus everywhere I look*. During this life's journey, we may veer off, get off the road, get stuck, miss the turn, or end up some place we did not intend. Even so, our Heavenly Father is faithful to restore us back. Second Timothy 2:13 from the English Standard Version states it this way, "If we are faithless, he remains faithful."

Hallelujah! Our Heavenly Father desires that none should perish. Hold on to Him and never let Him go. As a devout servant of the Lord I made regretful choices that landed me in prison. This is my personal experience of how the Lord administered His tough love to prepare me for the amazing work ahead. Jeremiah 29:11 NIV says, "For I know the plans I have for you, declares the Lord, plans to prosper you and not to harm you, plans to give you hope and a future." He will get us to where we are supposed to be, even if we stumble all the way. He gets us over the stumbling blocks that He already knew we would have.

Yes, in the midst of what was one of the most amazing times during my service in ministry, I made a wrong turn down what I thought was a one-way street with no outlets. I ignored all the warnings and flashing signs, violated all the principles I lived by, and didn't seek anyone's advice until I hit the barricade. I certainly did not expect to find myself in prison for three years and certainly not at the age of 50.

Step 3: Allow your stumbling blocks to become your stepping stones. Let them become the foundation upon which greatness can be built.

❧ CHAPTER 4 - GOOD INTENTIONS? NOT GOOD ENOUGH!

My good intentions became the justification for my actions. It's like selling drugs to build a community youth center. The end justifies the means. I thought since what I was doing didn't physically hurt anyone it was okay. I wasn't talking to anybody about this decision. I didn't have anyone to talk to and wouldn't have talked to them if I had. This can easily lead you into silence, being a leader, especially in ministry. It's not intentional. It just happens because people put you on a pedestal. There's no wiggle room. People expect you to be perfect. You are the standard. You can't make any mistakes. This makes it impossible to be vulnerable. Our failures become the secrets we silence. How can I give direction to someone else when my own moral compass is broken? I didn't spend much time thinking about the possible consequences; I had convinced myself there would be none. It was so important for me to preserve my image that I smiled right out of the office in handcuffs as far as my staff could see me. I could have saved myself some pain if I had followed Step 1: Be truthful.

It sounds so simple. Just tell the truth... but anyone who has *ever* had to face losing *everything* they have worked for knows that this can become far more complicated than it sounds. You can't get a $50,000 loan with 50 cents. When faced with getting or losing something we really want, we will often say or do whatever we think we have to do to win. Do you pray the Prayer of Invisibility? I used to. It's like when you're on a long road trip and you're getting tired. The "are we there yet" mantra is playing in your head. The speed limit is 70mph, but you're doing 80 or 90. That's when the "prayer of invisibility" comes in. You ask God to make your car invisible to all speed detection devices on land or air. You want to fly without penalty. I'm sure God laughs. I try putting it on cruise control but I can't take it when 10 cars speed past me. I know. You say, "You're a pastor. You're supposed to be an example." This is true. So are you, especially with that "Follow me as I follow Jesus" bumper sticker. I'm pushing 80 to keep up with you!

I use this to show how in one very simple way we deceive ourselves. The Word says to obey the law and yet I'm praying that He helps me successfully break it. And I don't want anybody to tell me it's wrong. That's how I know I'm in trouble: when I'm defending my wrong. "Well, I'm keeping up with traffic." In Atlanta 65mph feels like 50. The average speed is 80. It hasn't mattered much that the speed limit has been increased. It would have to be 70 in the city to keep pace.

Song of Solomon says it's the little foxes that spoil the vine. The little lies pave the way for big ones. They are the hardest to expose because they fall in the "everybody does it" category. These are the seeds that produce the fruit that is so difficult to uproot. It will take prayer for God to reveal the truth.

As one of my best friends (whom I deeply miss) would say, "leaving any of the details out of the story is lying!" Avoid that voice in your head that says it will work out. Even when things appear to be working out, it's still wrong if it didn't come from truth. There's no such thing as a "white lie." Fear had such a grip on me, I wouldn't even look at the truth. I just hung onto the voice saying, "It's going to work out for you. You'll make it right." I never tried telling the truth. My pride wouldn't allow me to hear the word "No." I wanted my unbroken record of "yes" to remain intact. Isn't that what a winner is? No matter how good your intentions are, if you aren't honest about everything including the pros and cons of the transaction, you are being deceptive. Being deceptive is dishonest. Dishonesty is devilish, and devilish is of the devil and against all of the principles of God. The way I negotiated in my mind, shutting everyone out of the process, almost caused me to self-destruct. My good intentions paired with the weeds of deception were self-destructive because I failed to pay attention to the flaws developing in my decision making ability. Each time the handling of problems grew larger and larger, I began to stretch my level of integrity to choices that caused me to dislike myself. I didn't identify with my need for help. I didn't know how to get help.

As an entrepreneur, I knew who and what I wanted to be like, but I didn't know the process, the answers, or how to hold to character when problems get harder and bigger. Living a life of integrity doesn't come with a manual. One would say, "Just don't do wrong." The reality is, everyone has violated integrity and character but many have the sense to stop when they realize the consequences, and then there are others who just don't get caught.

☞ CHAPTER 5 - THE BLESSING IS IN THE WAY

It was in the early hours of August 21, 2015, my beloved sister, the late Sylvia Nelson spoke these exact words in my dream, "The Blessing Is In The Way"! I anxiously wanted to know exactly what she was trying to tell me. I began to seek the Lord and He kept showing me the word *PATH* translated from the word *WAY*. Suddenly, everything I read for the next six months focused on the ways of the Lord. So every time I'd see the word *WAY* I would change it to say the *PATH*.

On January 4, 2016, nearing my seventh month in prison, while in the Career Center I was literally led by God to the library (which was in the same building). The Holy Spirit specifically led me to select a book to read for the week. I chose two, but the one I read first blew me away with the revelation I desperately needed before going home. The book is written by Pastor Andy Stanley and titled *The Principle Of The Path*. What an amazing and timely discovery! God could have allowed me to read it the first day. He could have allowed me to read it before I got in trouble, but He knew the day, place, and time He would allow Andy Stanley to pour into me! This was the day that my life changed forever! The principle of "the path" is the discovery of the knowledge that your today is connected to your tomorrow. Proverbs 3:5-6 states, "Trust in the Lord with all your heart, and do not lean on your own understanding. In all your ways acknowledge Him, and He will make straight your paths." The knowledge I gained from reading is what most of us fail to acknowledge. Once the principle of "the path" is discovered, we can use it to maximize our sense of direction. Just as you do not ignore the principles of gravity, you should not ignore the principles of "the path."

If you believe today is connected to tomorrow you must live like it. If you see the warning signs of trouble and keep going as if everything will work out somehow, you will end up in a place you didn't choose. Even when your intentions are good, when you make the wrong decisions, you will suffer the consequences because your destination has to be your compass, not your intentions.

The Principle of the Path spoke directly to my spirit! I was a classic example of what Pastor's book is about. I am a woman after God's own heart and I never had intentions to take anything from anyone, but I veered from the principles and made the wrong decisions that took me to a destination I did not choose.

What an amazing God to establish principles in the earth that don't discriminate! I know now that a simple change of direction will change my destination. Your choices determine your direction, and your direction determines your destination!

For example, if my goal is to win a gold medal running in track and field and I never go out to walk the track, much less jog or run, then my direction has determined my destination.

∽ CHAPTER 6 - PUSH PRIDE ASIDE

Leaders, Innovators, Artists, Professionals, Clergy, *everyone...* we need the help of others! If you are anything like I was and still working on it, you do not like to ask for help. Listen, someone once said, nothing of value is ever accomplished without the help of others. It's okay to ask for help! While we need people, partners, and relationships, we really need people we can share the deepest parts of our lives with. We need people that will hold us accountable, check on us, and most of all love us enough to tell us the truth. I hope you are not like I was. Do you help others but are too prideful to ask for help when you need it? Allow people to help you! Ask for help. We cannot, and I repeat, we cannot stand alone. Don't let pride trick you into going it alone because it tricked me! For many of us, asking for help is unthinkable. We go through life without experiencing the blessing of receiving help and deprive others the joy of giving us the help we so desperately need. To ask for help is not a weak thing. It's a smart thing.

There were many times the words *will you help me* would have saved me from pride. For example, I landed here in prison because I lied. I was untruthful to myself, and for the life of me I just could not ask for help. I didn't want anyone to think I needed them, so I lied. I crafted my lie to make me look good. Sound familiar? Maybe you can't fathom lying for something you felt you couldn't live without. Well the thought of my family, my friends, my business associates, and everyone else seeing me for who I had become had me bound. My pride had become so powerful that my business was literally paralyzed at the most crucial time of its existence. I stopped doing business and became consumed with this legal battle, a wrongful foreclosure suit that greatly impacted and torturously interfered with the business and every aspect of my life. Instead of asking for help from those whose guidance and support could have caused me to make informed decisions, I chose *shame, silence and secrets.*

Sometimes we simply do not have the answers, and it's okay. I didn't have the answer. Instead of being responsible, I allowed fear to drive me into irrational behavior. The fear of losing caused me to react instead of responding. I couldn't ask for help when I needed it the most. The situation got worse as I remained in denial. I really made a mess of so many things because I could not use the two words *help me.* You can pause right here and expose the fear of asking for help or if you need help, practice saying the words and go get your help!

Step 4: Ask for Help

ೞ CHAPTER 7 - TAKE AUTHORITY

TAKE authority! When I say take authority, I mean use your God given right to enforce your power over *shame, silence and secrets*. Let's pause together right here. Say this with me. "Shame, you are no longer welcome here! I command you to leave in Jesus name." Shame is not your friend, and it never will be. It disguises itself as a blanket of comfort, as a painkiller, and security by making you think it has the answer. It doesn't. In fact, it is a manipulator and an imitator of true genuine remorse. Shame is a thief, a cold-blooded murderer, a rapist and a liar. It can steal precious time, kill your desires to push through, and rape your creative mind.

Shame will literally wrap itself around pain and disguise itself as the answer. It leads you into delaying and denying yourself the victory. Shame says, "Don't tell!" It manipulates your mind to shut down, numb, cover up, and to walk away. When you are in shame, the enemy can leave you alone because you will destroy yourself. Shame has a tendency to put a grip on you that is hard to identify and even harder to break free of. Shame has a way of making you believe that what you are experiencing is your fault. It destroys people, relationships, ministries, and organizations in any place that it is allowed to form. Shame has manipulated more people into drugs, alcohol, prostitution and crime. It is seriously underrated. Shame can in no form or fashion lead us to a victorious result. Shame comes from fear and *"f.e.a.r.* is false evidence appearing real." After living with shame and being given the opportunity to face up and deal with the mistakes I had made, I chose freedom. Shame is no longer my man. He had to go!

Fear and shame are cousins. They must not be allowed to become terrorists. You cannot even give fear and shame an inch. Make this declaration with me, *"Fear and shame, I declare that your disguises are exposed and you are set free now, in the name of Jesus!"* Rise up and break the silence. We must share our stories to bring light into dark places. You are not alone. I stand with you and together we are delivered and walking in the freedom that Jesus Christ hung on the cross for!

May I share this from a business vantage point? Shame is always waiting for the opportunity to slip in when we fall short. It is true that failure is a part of the recipe for success. However, it does not have to result in shame. I'm so glad that the Wright brothers were not ashamed after they had failed many times to get planes to fly! The number of times they failed is staggering. If they had allowed shame to take over, there might never have been an airplane.

Don't allow shame, fear, or any negative thoughts to fester because those are evils that the enemy uses to destroy us. I declare, that you are more than a conqueror and no weapon formed against you shall prosper! *"I declare that you shall make the right choice now!"*

The self-desires that society promotes ultimately produce insecurity, narcissism, and self-promotion. These incubate in shame. Shame breeds, nurtures, grows, and amplifies. It drowns out every voice except your own. You die emotionally and spiritually because you disconnect. I remember people coming up to me sharing how they were blessed by my sermons while secretly I was living in shame, wearing it like a well-made garment that only I could see. I would downplay every compliment always giving my well-crafted disclaimer because I didn't feel worthy. During this time one of the Bishop's called me an angel and said I was a gift to the ministry, and in my mind I was thinking, "no... I am a devil." Those disclaimers were drawing more and more attention to who I was becoming. When I was experiencing this I was ashamed to stand out, ashamed to let go, ashamed of where I was, ashamed of what had happened, ashamed of this and ashamed of that. Leaders, this is a checkpoint! The truth is, shame's intention is to hold you hostage, keep you from moving forward, and to rob you of the great future that is ahead of you.

An 80-year-old woman hearing the *"shame"* discussion between my editor and I could not pass up the opportunity to share about her relationship with shame. She, too, had become a victim of shame and was "semi-crippled" as she called it. As a three-year-old she was kidnapped and molested repeatedly for two weeks. Though her circumstances were different, the result was the same. She lived captured in shame all her life. Like the walls of a cage, she was encased in it so much that everything in her life revolved around it. No matter how you get there, shame will cause you to be paralyzed. Crippled as a teenager until she was an adult, she experienced a pseudo self-guilt, a false humility. This shame affected everything and everyone she came in contact with. Even as an elderly adult she was so in its grip that she stayed in the house for months at a time. Because God can use anything, her shame became the catalyst He used for her freedom. When she finally opened up and talked about her experience, she accessed the power of God to break free from the shame. We last heard that she was out of the house enjoying life dining at a cafe.

I was a victim of shame when I lost my way, but the Lord would not allow me to remain paralyzed. He called me out. He used my shame. A lot of the Body of Christ has false humility. What had initially produced a false humility in me, God used to develop genuine humility. When we surrender our shame to Him, He will use it to drive us into our destiny. When you come into contact with shame don't stay there. Grab hold of your purpose. See yourself in the future. I see you. Your future is bright and you are winning.

Step 5: Surrender your fear and your shame. God will use them!

CHAPTER 8 - DO NOT DEVIATE

Deviation from the transformation process is a big mistake. When I surrendered myself to Fulton County Jail, I was still consumed with cleaning up my mess. My hope was to avoid the prison sentence that was already court ordered - but the prison sentence was a main part of the transformation process that lay ahead. I had it in my mind that somehow this was a mistake and God would help my lawyer to set me free. I had repented and I thought I was ready to go. A lot of us think that because we repent the consequences will be canceled. I deviated from the process and once again I gave fear and shame an open door to lie and manipulate me into thinking that the process was complete when it was really just beginning.

It is imperative that you acknowledge that there is a problem. Acknowledgment is the prerequisite for resolving our problems. If you do not first acknowledge that you have an issue, there will be no resolution. You also must acknowledge the problem the moment it shows up. It amazes me that, as a leader of a progressive ministry, I fell so short in the very early stages of pastoring the church I founded. I've never been so certain about anything in my life as I am about God calling Atlanta New Generation Ministry into existence! It was very perplexing to me that in the midst of the most profound time of ministry growth, I would succumb to pride and as a result create a reason to go prison. I remember thinking that I would not be sentenced to prison because God would not do that to the ministry, and certainly not those dedicated members. Listen carefully, He said to me, "I can stand still time and earth would never miss it!" I was not the only person on earth He could use as a vessel to lead Atlanta New Generation Ministries. Wow, in that moment I realized He had a major purpose for allowing prison to be a part of my transformation process. I also learned, in a Kairos moment, that He was restoring me at the same time He was preparing a People!

I was in the back seat of the Sheriff's car sitting in front of Lee Arrendale, a women's state prison. It was there that I was to begin physical diagnostics - a prerequisite to the ultimate prison sentence I was to serve. I did not realize that this was a parallel to the spiritual diagnostics I was to undergo. As I sat, I began to question my denial. I was so scared. I said to myself, "You've gotta look like you are not scared. You've gotta be brave." I remember walking into the cafeteria and staring at all the women. One of them said to me, "You look like you're lost. Come sit with us." I stood there in my white jumpsuit bewildered at having a glimpse of realization - prison had become a part of my journey.

I spent weeks at the state prison awaiting the ultimate. When I was finally transferred to Emanuel Women's Facility - the so-called "Cupcake Camp" - I was still keeping hope alive that I would have Divine intervention, an immediate release. One of the other ladies serving time received an immediate release. I was so happy for her because I just knew I was next. I spent hours and days waiting and looking for my moment. No one could tell me that my release was not in process.

As the days went by, my glimpse of realization became more formidable until the moment I went to a four-day retreat held by Kairos Prison Ministries. Let me show you how God works in our favor. I had not signed up for the retreat, but I was chosen. When I learned that my name was on the list to attend, I didn't even want to go. I did not think I needed it because I still thought I was going home. Everybody on the compound was talking about this spiritual retreat and how great it was. People had been waiting for years to be a participant. I had only been there a month and I was chosen - that's God's favor!

This retreat was tailored just for me. The retreat allowed me to cry every tear I needed to cry, forgive myself, forgive others, and be forgiven. I showed up feeling like I had only one breath left, not knowing what to expect, but with nothing to lose. Hope had to show up for me because I felt so incapable. It was as if I was a dead person walking. God allowed the volunteers of Kairos to pour so much of His love into us for those four days through the worship, fellowship, prayer, singing, and special ceremonies of forgiveness with object lessons that brought true deliverance. It was the beginning of the newfound perspective that facilitated my transformation process. I was in denial no more.

Step 6: Submit to the process!

ℭℨ CHAPTER 9 - THE BREAKING POINT

One of my major downfalls was the refusal to acknowledge my problem - keeping silent. The indicators of our behavior changes should be seen most clearly by the people that know us best. Our relationships are dysfunctional if our family and friends ignore us when we are acting out of character. However, I performed so well that I should have gotten an Academy Award. To my knowledge, no one noticed. Because of one problem that had many solutions, I shut down. Pride took over and I tried to handle it all by myself. I made more and more of a mess every time I touched the problem because at that time I did not refer to it as a problem. I was well-resourced to make things go away at my desire. My silence was my secret weapon - it helped me to cope by covering up everything I was feeling and everything I was facing. It allowed people to see only what I wanted them to see for some time. I didn't know how to fix the situation so silence was convenient while I was trying to figure out a solution.

Have you ever been broken? I have. After I left the Kairos retreat, I began to seek God specifically for His assignments while I was in prison. Interestingly enough, my assigned detail (job) was in the Chaplain's office. I was the inventory keeper of the indigent supplies and she gave me delegated authority to lead the women's ministry in her absence. I had no idea that her absence would be a significant amount of time. I also worked for the Chief Counselor. She was very impactful. God strategically placed her in my path because her standards were so high. She was a good model. God had just finished drilling the importance of principles in me as I read the book *The Principle of the Path*. God knew the woman I was to become required a different kind of brokenness to serve at the level He had designed me. This brokenness had to start on the inside in places I had protected for so long. I received the ultimate upgrade during my transformation and He did not leave a stone unturned. The accountability I experienced under the tutelage of the Chief Counselor, along with the opportunities afforded me by the Chaplain, shattered every desire that I had to keep quiet. Silence was no longer golden for me. This was God's real "breaking point." Like the olive, I was broken and crushed so the oil could flow.

We respond with confidence when we know the Lord, but when we do not know Him, we become unglued and submit to reacting instead of responding. Let me tell you, all of us have something in our lives that can potentially push us to a "breaking point." I have good news for you. What the enemy will use as a weapon, God will use as a tool. God will give us a response in the place of a reaction and cause us to triumph if we look to Him. Now, you are probably thinking, looking to God is easier said than done. Sure it is… before you come to know Him.

Are you at a "breaking point?" Are you forced to react to a devastating incident? Are you at a point of a major life decision? Is there an addiction that is costing you everything or is there a secret about something or someone in your life that has literally paralyzed you, numbed you, or caused you to tell lie after lie? When we feel like we must lie, that's the first sign of trouble. When we are going through extremes to keep something secret and we begin to isolate ourselves from others, that's a sign of trouble. Are you trying to resolve a problem, but the harder you try, the worse it gets? Or perhaps something happened that threatens everything you've accumulated. Do you feel like you are on the verge of snapping? Or maybe you have fallen off a cliff. I understand. I know now that I snapped - the kind of snap that causes unspiritual behavior. That snapping can foster in us a pattern of bad choices that seemingly will bring resolution, but in fact result in disaster and self-destruction.

My good intentions did not have a good outcome. The remnants of shame paralyzed and isolated me. My silence covered up my problems. I was always in damage control mode. It may be sad to say, but I was relieved when I went to prison because I didn't have to lie anymore. The hand of shame and guilt could no longer haunt me. I was relieved from the pressure to perform under the microscope of perfection. I did not have to hide in silence but could now shout from the rooftops of how God had helped me.

People put leaders on a pedestal and say to them, "Do not fail us." So, many of us have allowed this challenge of the pedestal to consume us and have found ourselves in a position where we feel we can't "ask" for help. With the help of a therapist and the aid of my prison experience, I realize that once our judgment becomes cloudy, our ability to make sound choices is distorted. The choices I made and the behavior patterns that lead me to disaster initially went unnoticed. I had reached a "breaking point" that clouded my ability to have sound judgment. That "breaking point" ultimately became beneficial because it led to taking full responsibility for my actions and submitting to an accountability process that I and everyone I come into contact with in the future will benefit from. When we submit and allow the "breaking point" to produce brokenness, we can live in freedom. Understand that God will never allow preparation to be wasted and He won't allow His investment in you to languish. Freedom awaits your arrival!

Step 7: Embrace the breaking. It is a necessary step towards freedom.

‰ CHAPTER 10 - FROM SPIRIT TO SPIRIT

Let me speak to your spirit! We are spiritual beings. These mortal bodies are the vehicles that are designed to mobilize and house our spirits, our temples. What shape are you in spiritually? Are you spiritually fit? Can you pass the test? It's normal to react with a natural response, but the Lord calls us to a supernatural response like, "turn the other cheek," and, "to love our enemies." While we are all under construction and have room for improvement, now is an excellent time to self-evaluate and apply reinforcement where needed to make sure we are strong enough to withstand the storms. Although things that happen in life appear to happen to our bodies, they ultimately attack our spirit because our spirit is who we really are. If our spirit is intact, which can only be if we are walking with Him, we are more inclined to be aware of when a storm is approaching. To walk with Him is to be in agreement with His Word that loads us with benefits. We need the benefits afforded us through being in agreement with His Word. Please understand that the storms that come are designed by our adversary to take us out. Remember, we wrestle not against flesh and blood, but against powers, spiritual wickedness and principalities. Lord, we thank you for the power that you have given us to overcome all the wiles of the devil.

Let me bring more enlightenment from a lesson that I learned in a very hard and expensive way. I wrote of this briefly in a previous chapter. I want to tell you the entire story. I believe it will help you. Keep your spirit in ready condition because it is so critical to be positioned in the time of attack! As I was nearing fifty years old, I thought I had it all together until, in what seemed to me at the time to be a catastrophe, a financial institution (of whom I am legally bound to not name) showed up on my doorstep! After more than twenty years of success in a "male-dominated business," I was suddenly confronted with multiple wrongful foreclosure claims against all of my commercial properties. Due to the bank's accounting error (and their lack of accountability), I was accused of defaulting on payments. I felt violated and betrayed. To help you understand how much this hurt, I must fully disclose the depth of our banking relationship. I went from being able to call the bank and within 24 hours getting hundreds of thousands of dollars moved to the account of my choice, to sitting in a property I had financed through the bank that they claimed was no longer mine (and I didn't know it). When I finally found out the relationship I thought I had was clearly an arrangement that had changed just like the weather, I snapped.

When I should have cried out for help and direction from God, I reacted instead and went straight to the courthouse. Filing a lawsuit wasn't a bad thing, but I didn't seek counsel or directions from God. I acted completely out of rage and primal instinct. Had my spiritual condition been intact, the outcome would have been different. I was spiritually and emotionally vulnerable, so when the bank foreclosures were filed against me, my mind, will and volition were compelled to punch back. I had great responsibilities at church. I still had major deals on the table with my company. Because I felt like I needed to save the business for my family and my employees, I kindly stepped into the role of savior. I was unaware that I had fallen off a cliff and I began to function outside of the principles that I stood for. In the privacy of my own secret self, I began making decisions in a cloak-and-dagger type of way that set me on a path to prison where they gladly received me.

I was so paralyzed that I became a person functioning from day to day with secrets that manipulated my very existence. These secrets created in me a desire to fight by whatever means necessary. I was not going to allow that bank to take apart what my sisters and I had spent years building. Here, I want to shed light on how we can slip into what I call "Paralyzed Silence" with a single thought, one focus to fight a battle that could not be won the way we think it should be won and without God's direction.

When this horrible thing threatened the image of our business, a pillar in the community, the award winning DBABS Construction, Inc., I was furious. When I reflect back, I realize that the neglect of my own spiritual nourishment left me open to react with the mind of a delusional threatened person. I was wrong and I desire to prevent others from making the same mistakes I made. I was trusting in the bank. I was trusting in the attorneys. I was trusting in my employees. I was trusting in the courts. However, when everything went awry, I had problems trusting in God. And it was God who raised up a people who defended my company and got results without the courts, attorneys, and me. It was a happy day when our properties were finally returned to us.

Step 8: Trust GOD first! Only He can do what no one else can do.

❧ CHAPTER 11 - DRIVEN

What's driving you and where will it take you? Stop, look, and listen! It's important to know the answer to the questions up front. Don't assume. You may be moving in a direction that leads to a dead end. Smart up!

I was so driven to build an empire and I "knew" I was moving in the right direction. No one could tell me a thing. I put everything else to the back of the line; getting married, having children, family gatherings, vacations, entertainment and non-business affairs literally took a back seat for over twenty years of my life. Early in life I dreamed of building a Fortune 500 business. It was all I ever wanted.

It's amazing how we allow the wrong people to attach to our dreams so freely. At first I thought of them as leeches sucking the blood right out of me, but later I realized they were parasites who were sucking me dry from the inside and I did not know it. I was equally as amazed by how I seemed to move through life, running into obstacles that caused a delay or alteration in my plan. The decisions you make as a result of this kind of behavior ensure that many of life's lessons are learned the hard way. There are Godly principles and systems in place to teach us. We must work smarter, not harder. Many of us never research or inquire how we can work smarter. We are so naive when we think we have all the answers. We are so eager to reinvent the wheel. King Solomon asked for wisdom. A lot of us never ask for wisdom until we run into a brick wall for the second or third time. Sometimes we have to run into it so hard until we knock ourselves unconscious. No matter how much we already know, there is always some wisdom and knowledge we will need to seek out. Lord, grant me strength to do what I must, knowledge to understand Your principles, and the wisdom to apply them.

The worst thing that can ever happen is for us to think that we have arrived. If we are not prepared for opportunities when they come, we will be like the five foolish virgins in the Bible (and me) who were not prepared for the bridegroom and missed the wedding. Let me encourage you to take an honest assessment right now. It is so important to know where you are. Are you the person who can't see the trees because you are so deep in the forest. Can you even smell the honeysuckle or the roses or are you in too deep? If we are prepared, we will respond with actions and informed choices that are in line with Godly principles. This will advance us to the place in life that God has waiting for us.

I had an overabundance of opportunity, but I could not take advantage of it. I didn't take time to appreciate all that I was so blessed with. I was so caught up thinking I was *on point*, but it turns out that I was *off* because I was chasing more. The "more you have the more you want" syndrome is a way of life in our society. I know because I've had the chance to step away from the rat race. It literally and secretly had wrapped itself around me. I was consumed and blinded by it all. My company had become the lifeblood for so many others who had surrendered their licenses in the mortgage and insurance collapse of 2008. There were companies who lost everything and attached themselves to us so could they could survive. I did not realize that I had accumulated an obsession to maintain an image 24/7 for at least five years before falling off the cliff. They became our subcontractors or vendors, and I felt responsible for them.

Something happened in 2013 when I was in my prime as a female double-minority specialized government contractor and while having the honor of being installed as Senior Pastor of a mature and stable community church - I began to see myself in the image I created. That image afforded me the false belief that people loved me. But did they really love me? In actuality, they loved what being connected to me afforded them. That's why it is imperative to perform a self-check up and to know why people are in your life. It's okay for people to want something from you, but it's the hidden agendas that will destroy relationships.

After everything I have lived through, I practice being translucent - clear. Now that I have a mentor I am open and put everything on the table. We all need something from each other. God created us to need each other. Sometimes we are embarrassed when we need someone. We think it means that we have a deficiency. It's not a deficiency at all. It's a space God created to force us to reach out. We get in the most trouble trying to be totally self-sufficient. Just be clear and up front. It eliminates the work of Satan. Make clarity a fully active component in your life. Clarity eliminates confusion. You may not admit this, but it's true when you really think about it. We all need an accountability partner. This is mutually beneficial. It increases the value of our relationships.

❄ CHAPTER 12 - FREEDOM

ARE you walking in freedom? The ability to walk in freedom was created for God's people, but many of us have allowed fear to imprison us instead. We assume we know what freedom is. Freedom is so ambiguous. Let's take a moment to define what it really is. For those who have been incarcerated, it means having the ability to go where you choose to go. It's also as simple as getting up when you want to get up. Freedom is simply free agency. It is the power or right to go as you please.

Freedom affects those who have never spent a day in prison in the same way that it affects those of us who have. Let's not be superficial when we look at this. Freedom has to be more than having things. Our society tells us that freedom is financial and accompanies a status that we often get in debt to achieve. Debt is bondage - just another type of prison. I don't think it should come as any surprise that I started seeing things from a financial perspective when that is what was responsible for me going to prison in the first place. This reminds me of the scripture that says, (James 4:3 KJV) "You ask and do not receive, because you ask with wrong motives, so that you may spend it on your pleasures." This is the total definition of freedom for some people and for our society. We have been sold a bill of goods through advertising. Society says that freedom is the ability to get more. We spend our entire lives getting more, thinking that this is our freedom, and then we protect our ability to get more with our very lives. If your life is consumed with having more things, you will always be imprisoned by your choices and not ever thinking about spending wisely. By the way, we are not just talking about our money, but we are also talking about our time.

When we evaluate freedom, we need to be aware that it ultimately becomes the power to have equal opportunity to live independently without hindrance. However, freedom comes with responsibility. What does freedom look like to you? Everyone needs to answer that question for themselves. If we learn to appreciate the "now," we will find freedom in every step we take. Oh, if we only knew how adequately supplied we are in the now!

Fear is an enemy of freedom. It manipulates you to think that you don't have enough. Through false senses of thirst, hunger, desperation, and lack, we drink from the fountain of fear. Fear grips us with lies and deception. It is the opposite of Faith. Faith in God gives us a promise, hope, and an assurance. We must secure the promises of God, live in faith, and accept the victorious life that is a benefit of belonging to Him! Who would have thought freedom could come from a prison experience! We now know that God can cause freedom to come from any place.

Allow Jesus to set you free. If you know Him, repent and live in freedom. If you do not know Him, I encourage you to invite Him into your heart. Pray this prayer with me: "Father, I know that I have broken your laws and my sins have separated me from you. I am truly sorry, and now I want to turn away from my past sinful life toward you. Please forgive me, and help me avoid sinning again. I believe that Your son, Jesus Christ, died for my sins, was resurrected from the dead, is alive, and hears my prayer. I invite Jesus to become the Lord of my life, to rule and reign in my heart from this day forward. Please send your Holy Spirit to help me obey You, and to do Your will for the rest of my life. In Jesus' name I pray, Amen."

Step 9: Allow Jesus to set you free.

❧ CHAPTER 13 - WHO'S WITH ME?

As the late Sylvia Nelson, my baby sister, would say, "Who's with me?" Some people are just not with you no matter what you do or how you try. Many of our associates were hitchhikers, dream killers, and thieves. They didn't want to go anywhere, and they definitely didn't want us to go anywhere. The thieves would rather ride with you long enough to steal your vision, rob you of your energy, and show up later as your competition. Then there are other people who aren't meant to go where you're going. So when the shakedown comes, (I call it Divine intervention), *let them go* and you go with that flow. When you learn who's not with you, don't be discouraged. Be very encouraged! The best thing we could ever learn from this life's lesson is *who is with us!*

For some reason, my baby sister, Sylvia would say to me constantly, "Folks will ride in your limo but when you ride the bus, they will not be there." She was so right. I am so grateful to come into the knowledge of what it really means to stand with someone. Loyalty is in my DNA. Perhaps my loyalty to others may have somehow been a downfall. Even when they were not loyal to me, I was loyal to them. There are those who could never understand why I continue to give people the benefit of the doubt. Is there a line drawn to limit loyalty, if so where should that line be drawn? At what point do you not extend your loyalty? When I say "I am with you," I mean it. But many people are with you only when it's good for them.

So how do you know that people are with you? A lot of times it may appear that people are with you because they show glimpses of sincere commitment. But are they really loyal? Loyalty is tested by fire. It's when the project is almost done and you are close to your deadline but you need someone to stay. Everyone has already worked 12 -15 hours. Everybody wants to go home. Mr. Loyal will stay without complaint. He will not allow other commitments to take precedence. A person who is loyal is firmly established because of the relationship you share. There is a difference between loyalty and commitment. A person can make a decision to be committed without ever having a relationship with you. It's just a decision and that decision can be motivated and changed like the weather.

Loyalty is most tested in difficult situations. Before Sylvia went to be with the Lord, she stressed to me that the things I was going through were necessary and a part of my journey. Just as there was a cup for Jesus, there is a cup for us. What I am referring to is the time when Jesus was in the Garden of Gethsemane. Loyalty was being tested both ways - first, His loyalty to the Father, and second, the Disciples' loyalty to Him. He knew that He was going to have to die on the cross.

He also knew that Judas was going to betray Him. That was His cup. Prison was mine. You also have yours. Jesus asked His Father if He must drink from this cup? I begged God not to allow me to experience prison and even when He did, I continued to beg Him every day until I finally surrendered to His will. There was never a day I didn't want to come home. He knew it. Because of our loving Father's relationship with us, He continues to demonstrate His loyalty even when we haven't been loyal to Him. He hears, feels, and knows our pain and delivers us from it. He is always in control, and He knew the day that He would open the gates for me to walk freely from the prison!

The most painful part of prison was the unaccepted phone calls from people I thought would never leave me. Sometimes I would call again saying, "Surely they are going to answer the phone." They didn't. Three years later they still aren't answering. I had to redefine what it means to be loyal. These are the people I put myself on the cross for, but they walked all over my blood. My sacrifices meant nothing, but before prison no one could have convinced me that they were not loyal. I thought nothing would ever separate us. I know that my relationship with the Lord is stronger than it has ever been. The old Brunetta would have said, "I'm going to keep to myself. I'm not going to tell these people about my weaknesses. They hurt me." Now I trust God. I am allowing

Him to bring people into my life. People who I would never have had anything to do with are now my friends. I don't worry about who's with me anymore. I trust God.

✂ CHAPTER 14 - STRETCH ME LORD

There are time slots in God's plan for our lives during which He will stretch us and prune us to cause us to produce more fruit. There is a common phrase that I believe applies here - no pain, no gain. God trains us, builds us, and grows us. When we come to know Him and trust Him with our lives, we will find ourselves yielding to Him. Lord stretch me! I remember my spiritual mentor talking about God stretching him and, in my mind, I thought, "stretch me like a rubber-band that pops? ...not me." I did not want to comprehend those words. Why would anyone volunteer to be stretched - especially if it felt like what it looked like? Honestly, at that time, it sounded pretty painful... and I have come to know that it is. But, the end result will not disappoint you! I want to reiterate, no pain, no gain.

From my experience, stretching for a human being is very much like pruning for a tree. When a tree is pruned, it is clipped by its branches and it even looks painful, but this important part of the process is required for a tree to bear more fruit. When we allow the Lord to guide us through traumatic experiences, we become more understanding, patient, caring, and are more sensitive to the Lord. Experiencing prison made me more compassionate, forgiving, patient and it also exposed me to the many different personalities and problems others face. It gave me a broadened perspective about life and people as it relates to God's love for all of us. What an amazing opportunity to be used by God for His glory! If God never stretches us, we will never grow and see the beauty of our ashes.

I began to fall in love with God just before I received my first appointment as pastor of a fifty-year-old ministry. It's one thing to love the Lord, but it is a totally different experience to fall in love with Him. My desire escalated from the duties of my walk as a Christian to a desire to walk in agreement with Him! Yes, I found myself incarcerated after I had committed the crime that would ultimately send me to prison. However, it was during this love affair that God began to stretch me. I continue to mention my incarceration because I realize it was a major component with many of the pieces that would expand the ministry that God has placed in me. Of course, I was furious about prison. I kicked, screamed and hollered, but the moment I stopped, God began to show me how stretching would make me taller, broaden my perspective, and deepen my commitment to purpose! He began to minister to me in a way that only He can. The pain began to take a back seat as I began to see the plan, purpose, and promise of God come forth in my life.

I remember that when I began surrendering to Him fully, I

stopped focusing on the day I would be set free from prison. I realized that He would begin to release the keys to freedom to me as I surrendered myself to Him. We were all made for His purpose. I love the way He deals with us right where we are. No one can chastise and love you like He does! He promised to use everything that we have experienced for His purpose in our lives.

Step 10: Allow yourself to be stretched.

ℭ CHAPTER 15 - RESET AND REPOSITION

It is time to refresh! Turn the page. Walk into your due season. It's your turn "now" to receive the blessings in scripture that add no sorrow. The lessons you have learned and the experiences you have had are a part of your equipping and training. If you never allow preparation to be wasted, you can look forward to the blessings of God that will chase you down and overtake you! Remember that opposition comes with opportunity. If you have followed the previous steps, you are prepared to face opposition. Our God is so amazing. He carries us while we are going through the most challenging of trials and tribulations. He corrects us with such a loving touch. You have to know that the only reason God will allow you such unprecedented pressure is so that you can fulfill your purpose. You have a treasure inside of you. Like the diamond, it can only be produced by pressure. Like the pearl, the irritation you experience brings forth beauty. Given the opportunity, we would never choose pressure or irritation but God uses these to push us into our purpose.

What a powerful moment when God hits the reset button. It's like when we are using our computer and the screen freezes. We try everything that we can think of because we don't want to lose our document. Finally, after trying everything, the only solution is to hit the reset button. It appears that we may have lost it all. Having the opportunity to rewrite it makes it better than it was before. It is just like that for us in life. Suddenly in the midst of doing it our way, God presses the reset button. We didn't even know that option was available. His reset button is customized for each one of us. He is refining the details so that when we are reset our eyes are open to His will. We can see the path. It is a whole new life that is greater than before.

I was finally ready for repositioning, so God sat me down in prison. He had to delete my old mindset. I thought I was God! I had no idea the plans He had for me. Sure, I had confessed them. There is a huge difference between knowing and understanding. There is also a huge difference between saying and doing. When the word says be a doer and not just a hearer, I had to learn to apply it. Leaders must especially seek the Lord. There is so much to learn about Him. Though our search will continue for a lifetime, the search gets sweeter and sweeter as the days go by.

Another part of my repositioning included expansion of my territory. God expanded my vision from constructing buildings to becoming His co-laborer in constructing all aspects of a person's life. Part of the reset was recognizing God is the only SOVEREIGN and repositioning myself as servant. At the end of our lives, the greatest compliment we can ever receive comes from God when He says, "**Well done, good and faithful servant**; you have been **faithful** over a few things, I will make you ruler over many things. Enter into the joy of your Lord" (Matthew 25:16-23 emphasis added).

Step 11: Don't be afraid to let God press the reset button. Your life will always be better than it was before.

❧ CHAPTER 16 - HE STILL LOVES ME

In the next book, "HE STILL LOVES ME," I will share in depth about prison, and how it turned out to be my "Joseph moment." Joseph, a person in the Bible, was the favorite son of his father. By giving him gifts that showed he was the most loved son, he created intense jealousy among the brothers. They hated him. Although there are many differences between my life and Joseph's, our experiences are very much alike. You don't want to miss it!

This book is based on real life experience. I did not dream a moment of it. I paid for it for three years in tears. I am learning to apply God's word in every situation. Follow the steps and you, too, will arrive at your appointed destination. I owe everything to God for His mercy, grace, patience, and love. He's real but don't get it twisted. I was stripped naked and He still loves me and uses me for His glory! I'm so glad He's not like us. He doesn't write us off when we mess up. I declare that no matter where you are in life, and whatever you have done, God is waiting for you to let Him help. You are never useless. He specially designed your experience so you would be ready for the purpose He designed just for you.

God's help looked a lot different from what I wanted, but I now know that it was the help He chose for me. When I realized I had made some of the worst mistakes in my life, it took some time for me to realize I needed the "super" to collide with the "natural." Get this, I tried to tell God how to help me, which did not include the pain and suffering. He was not going for it. In fact, everything I told Him not to do, He did. I had to learn He is best at giving directions and I had to learn how to take them.

The major point of the lesson is to never become complacent or think you can make right out of wrong. It is imperative to keep watch over your spirit daily. Scripture says, "Put on the full armor of God so that we may stand against the wiles of the evil one." Nothing angers the enemy more than a fully equipped saint that is actively pursuing God. I was fully active as the leader of a very progressive ministry and a well-established business, but at some point I got lost! Warning: Be sure to line up all your dealings with Godly principles. Do not deviate one inch. My mistake was not being truthful.

Come clean *now* because the Father already knows. Close the door to *shame, silence, and secrets* because they will always lead you to self-destruction. The people you care about the most will be the people that will suffer the most. Whatever you are going through, whatever you have done, stop today and move in the right direction of confession and truth. It may seem like there is another way out, but I know firsthand there is not.

There may be some consequences, but you are better off taking care of it now than if you wait until later. I know because the more I tried to fix the problems silently and secretly, the more mess I created. Let me help you, your future is brighter than you think! I declare that you shall receive the strength, courage, and wisdom you need to make the right choice now, in Jesus name! Amen!

Step 12: Live the life God prepared just for you.

The Steps:

Step 1: Be Truthful

Step 2: Find yourself a Mentor, find a Coach, or find an Adviser that has achieved your goal, or is at a minimum actively doing the work.

Step 3: Allow your stumbling blocks to become your stepping stones. Let them become the foundation upon which greatness can be built.

Step 4: Ask for Help

Step 5: Surrender your fear and your shame. God will use them!

Step 6: Submit to the process!

Step 7: Embrace the breaking. It is a necessary step towards freedom.

Step 8: Trust GOD first! Only He can do what no one else can do.

Step 9: Allow Jesus to set you free.

Step 10: Allow yourself to be stretched.

Step 11: Don't be afraid to let God press the reset button. Your life will always be better than it was before.

Step 12: Live the life God prepared for you.

ொ THE AUTHOR - PASTOR BRUNETTA NELSON

Pastor Brunetta Nelson is the seventh child of the late Alphonzo Nelson & Pastor Doris Nelson. Pastor Brunetta Nelson is the Chief Executive of Imprint Productions, Inc. and the former owner of DBABS Construction, Inc. She is an Author, Public Speaker, and a Community Activist. Pastor loves the work of the Lord, her family, all people with an extraordinary passion for the young people. She is truly a woman after God's heart. Her favorite scripture is Proverbs 23:7, For as he thinketh in his heart, so is he!

Pastor Nelson earned her Degree in Journalism, as well as numerous government continued education certifications at the local, state and Federal level. Pastor Nelson is preparing to extend her ministerial training at The International Theological Center in Atlanta Georgia. She is a life-long learner, educator and Corporate Member of National Association of Women Owned Small Businesses and so many others.

Pastor Nelson accepted the Lord as her Savior in 1985. She was later called to preach in 1992 and later ordained as an Elder. She began her training at Christian Family Worship Center under the leadership of Bishop Joseph L. Price. Pastor Nelson served as Christian Family Worship Center's Sunday

School Superintendent for several years before she was promoted into an executive role. Pastor Nelson was installed as Pastor of Christian Family Worship Center on May 26, 2013. Pastor Nelson is passionate about the Lord and His work. She was given clear and precise instructions from God, to take care of His business and He will take care of hers.

On September 4, 2014 Pastor founded Atlanta New Generation Ministries, Inc. The ministry doubled and continued growing until a moment of tragedy happened that would change the immediate course of Pastor's direction. Pastor's business would come under attack at the most unexpected time. Under enormous pressure, Pastor made a choice that resulted in three years of state prison. Her story is the epitome of how God produces a message from a mess. God placed pastor on His fast track list of recovery. The new charge God has given pastor includes a brand-new ministry, business, a host of new associates & friends, and a community minds to imprint and impact every person and thing she comes in contact with.

Made in the USA
Columbia, SC
10 July 2019